FAKE NEWS
AND THE
FACTORIES
THAT
MAKE IT

Kristina Lyn Heitkamp

Enslow Publishing
101 W. 23rd Street
Suite 240
New York, NY 10011
USA
enslow.com

Published in 2019 by Enslow Publishing, LLC.
101 W. 23rd Street, Suite 240, New York, NY 10011

Library of Congress Cataloging-in-Publication Data

Names: Heitkamp, Kristina Lyn, author.
Title: Fake news and the factories that make it / Kristina Lyn Heitkamp.
Description: New York : Enslow Publishing, 2019. | Series: Critical thinking about digital media | Includes bibliographical references and index. | Audience: Grades 7-12.
Identifiers: LCCN 2018016413| ISBN 9781978504721 (library bound) | ISBN 9781978505674 (pbk.)
Subjects: LCSH: Fake news—Juvenile literature. | Journalism—History—21st century—Juvenile literature. | Online journalism—Juvenile literature.
Classification: LCC PN4784.F27 H45 2018 | DDC 070.4/3--dc23
LC record available at https://lccn.loc.gov/2018016413

Printed in the United States of America

To Our Readers: We have done our best to make sure all websites in this book were active and appropriate when we went to press. However, the author and the publisher have no control over and assume no liability for the material available on those websites or on any websites they may link to. Any comments or suggestions can be sent by email to customerservice@enslow.com.

Photo Credits: Cover, p. 1 (silhouette) Mads Perch/DigitalVision/Getty Images; cover, p. 1 (background) zorbital/Shutterstock.com; p. 8 Blend Images/Shutterstock.com; p. 10 goodluz/Shutterstock.com; p. 13 Everett Historical/Shutterstock.com; p. 16 Brian A Jackson/Shutterstock.com; p. 19 Universal Images Group/Getty Images; pp. 21, 26, 46 © AP Images; p. 25 Bloomberg/Getty Images; p. 30 The Photo Works/Alamy Stock Photo; p. 33 Sipa USA/AP Images; p. 36 Zoonar GmbH/Alamy Stock Photo; p. 39 NetPhotos/Alamy Stock Photo; p. 42 Kuttig - People 2/Alamy Stock Photo; p. 44 NASA/Hulton Archive/Getty Images; p. 48 Scott Olson/Getty Images; p. 51 Bloomicon/Shutterstock.com; p. 53 vvoe/Shutterstock.com; p. 56 Rawpixel.com/Shutterstock.com; p. 58 metamorworks/Shutterstock.com; p. 61 Wayhome Studio/Shutterstock.com; p. 63 Alain Bommenel, Sabrina Blanchard, Jonathan Jacobsen AFP/Newscom; lightbulb icon okili77/Shutterstock.com.

CONTENTS

INTRODUCTION

On November 9, 2016, Eric Tucker left a meeting near downtown Austin, Texas. It was an overcast and foggy day in the capital city. As he made his way home, Tucker saw something that made him stop. Dozens of buses lined up along the street. The fleet of buses could've easily held at least a couple hundred people. Tucker took out his phone, snapped a few photos, and went on his way.

When Tucker arrived home, he did a little investigating. After a cursory Google search, he came to the assumption that the buses were not for people attending a local event or conference but for paid protestors carted in to demonstrate against the controversial election of President Donald Trump. He had seen news coverage of protestors located just a few blocks from where he had taken the photos. Tucker decided to share the revelation with his whopping forty followers on Twitter. He posted three images on the social media platform with the caption: "Anti-Trump protesters in Austin today are not as organic as they seem. Here are the busses [sic] they came in. #fakeprotests #trump2016 #austin"

Little did Tucker know his tweet would go viral in a matter of hours and spark a massive conspiracy theory that still lingers. Less than ten hours later, Tucker's tweet was posted on the Reddit community of supporters for Donald Trump. The title of the post read: "BREAKING: They found the buses! Dozens lined up just blocks away from the Austin protest." Pro-Trump and right-leaning websites were on the story immediately. The post was quickly shared and received over 300 comments. Tucker's tweet was retweeted over 16,000 times and shared on Facebook over 350,000 times. A local Fox News channel picked up the story, as well as the conservative website Gateway Pundit.

What were the buses really doing there? The buses were for a data software conference. After making local and national news, it turned out to be a deliciously false story that was served up across several social media platforms and websites. The media called out Tucker, and he deleted the tweet. He apologized and retweeted the original tweet with "false" stamped across it. However, his confession wasn't nearly as popular, only getting a few shares and fewer than one hundred likes.

Moral of the true story—fake news is enticing. Some Americans salivate for a juicy story, true or false. The modern world is tightly knit and extremely connected, so just about anybody can spread misinformation. The architect behind fake news doesn't have to be a Russian troll or political campaigner—she or he can be an average person who jumps to conclusions without critically evaluating the situation.

In recent years, bogus news has ambushed our media streams. It's challenging to identify the shape-shifting beasts as they lurk among our communications. The first step in the battling fake news is to own our responsibility. As news consumers, it is our duty to critically evaluate articles, sources, and sensational front-webpage clickbait. Don't become a passive gossip, sharing scandalous headlines as truth. Fake news can suck the marrow from public discourse and the foundation of democracy. Phony stories will continue to plague our communications, and it is essential to arm yourself with the tools to fight for the truth.

In the Newsroom

People read it on smartphones. They peruse it on the black-and-white pages of a daily newspaper, or tune into TV's talking heads to hear the latest news.

The exchange of information is one of the oldest and most important human enterprises. The executive director of Columbia Links, a high school journalism, news literacy, and leadership program in Chicago for at-risk teens, Brenda Butler succinctly describes news storytelling. "Journalism is for the people. It is community-centric yet global in perspective. It is to inform and enlighten; to expand the dialogue; to probe and provoke; to stimulate and engage; to show the way or present another way; to open the doors and to uncover wrong; to give the voiceless a megaphone."[1]

After the Fact

At the most basic level, journalism is there to bear witness of events. A crime beat reporter will rush to the scene of a gruesome murder to gather details. War correspondents brave conflict zones to cover stories from the front line. Foreign correspondents enter the field to reveal human tragedy.

The purpose of journalism is to inform, not entertain or deceive, but in this modern era of fake news reports, how can you tell one from the other? It takes a critical eye and a logical mind to confirm sources.

Journalism also holds power to account. Often recognized as the fourth estate, the free press is essential in any democratic society. British political thinker Edmund Burke reportedly said that there were three traditional branches of government—the legislative, executive, and judicial. But that "the Reporters Gallery yonder, there sat a fourth Estate more important far than they all."[2] The free press is the watchdog, the keeper of accountability, and the system of checks and balances.

Investigative news can reveal hidden information, such as corruption, election interference, or when businesses break rules. Being informed is an important part of a democratic society. If a country's citizens are primed, they can have a knowledgeable voice in how their government is run.

A news story should answer questions. A well-written and researched story will reply to the questions who, what, where, when, why, and how. Not answering the appropriate questions will result in an incomplete story and a confused reader. For example, imagine if a reporter forgot to answer the *when* question while covering the Eric Tucker story. The event took place less than twenty-four hours after the election of Donald Trump—a notable time of mixed emotions and confusion. If a reporter neglected to evaluate the why, which explains the bigger context of the story, the reader may fail to critically evaluate the event.

In the Tucker story, the why helps the reader understand the consequences of spreading fake news and the damage caused by Tucker's assumption. Activists or concerned citizens are often falsely accused of being paid protestors. If a story doesn't cover all its bases, chances are it is either a poorly written piece or the story is purposely withholding information— either because it doesn't fit with the agenda or details weren't confirmed.

The Gatekeepers

Four factors determine which stories get pushed through to publication and which land on the cutting-room floor: the universal news drivers, editorial judgment, profits and competition, and reader judgment. Universal news drivers are the stuff that makes news stories sing. They give it value, and inspire readers to dive deep into an article or share widely with their community.

Each of these drivers also answers who, what, where, when, why, and how. The drivers turn information into news. There are ten universal news drivers[3]:

Fake news is shared more than actual news because it sounds sensational. Humans love drama and intrigue, so they're drawn right in. Verify your sources before you share with friends.

- Importance: information that the public needs to know, such as a school shooting or a wildfire.
- Prominence: information about public figures. For example, stories about politicians or celebrities.
- Human interest: stories about everyday people, like the local teen who raises thousands to benefit the homeless.
- Conflict: stories that cover conflict, like battles between Trump supporters and Clinton supporters.
- Change: alerts the reader to a big change, whether it's good or bad, opportunity or threat.
- Peculiarity: a story about the unusual, such as a cat that bites a dog.
- Magnitude: stories about data and surprising numbers, for example the hottest winter recorded.
- Proximity: local news.
- Timeliness: holidays, anniversaries, and stories that centerpiece the timely event.
- Relevance: a story with a big audience, such as an article about taxes being raised.

While a story about how a stray cat bit the mayor's dog during a fundraiser for the new community swimming pool is newsworthy, it still has to pass a few more gatekeepers to make headline. Editorial judgment is used to decide if the information is worthy of publishing. Editors of a news organization will try to find a balance between what readers want to read and what information they need to know—a good mix of both interesting stories and important stories. The editor pays attention to who reads the publication and what they like to read. For example, the magazine the *Economist* probably wouldn't include a photo story of what Justin Timberlake had for breakfast, nor would *People* publish a story about the trade war between the US and China.

Because news organizations are businesses that need to make money to pay for reporting and publication, competition and profits also guide news stories. Breaking news, the first to scoop a story, or having exclusive information from top-notch sources all drive news and influence the value and profits of news organizations. However, some may argue that competition in news markets could lead to an increase in sensationalized low-quality stories, where interesting always pummels importance.

The reader also plays a part in deciding what is newsworthy. In the new age of media, if a story is reblogged, retweeted, or shared, it adds value to the story. The power shifts from the editor to the reader. Readers want to know what everyone is reading. The most popular stories will sit front and center on many news organizations' websites. Reader judgment also curates their newsfeed. Mathematical formulas called algorithms tailor readers' newsfeeds based on which headlines they click on, the stories they share, and even the keywords they search for on the internet.

Framing the Narrative

News is presented in many forms, from traditional communication like print newspapers and TV news, to media convergence formats. Mass communication uses print, electronic, and

I Want YOU

The goal of journalism is to inform, whereas entertainment, such as a movie or book, is used to amuse or distract a person from daily life. Journalism uses verified and independent knowledge to empower readers, while entertainment uses actors and fantasy. But propaganda leads the consumer down a black hole. Propaganda muddies the media world by emotionally manipulating the reader with images and fallacious reasoning. The main goal of propaganda is to persuade the reader or viewer to a particular viewpoint. An infamous example of propaganda is the World War I poster of Uncle Sam pointing to the viewer exclaiming "I want YOU for the US Army."[4] The pointing finger is meant to intimidate and guilt new recruits into joining the war.

Uncle Sam wants you and will recruit you through intimidation if possible.

digital media. Print media includes newspapers, magazines, and books, while electronic media comprises TV and radio. Digital media uses a combination of computers, software, and networks to publish information. Media convergence is when you smash print, electronic, and digital media together, for example reading a *New York Times* article on a smartphone, or watching a political rally on a tablet. Digital media allows users to interact with news stories in a way that print or electronic media never could.

The evolving media landscape means readers, watchers, and listeners are consuming their news in many ways and from different platforms. According to a Pew Research Center survey, over half of Americans devour news on social media, including Facebook, Twitter, and Tumblr. Reddit was most popular, with 70 percent of users getting their news from the massive communication community, whereas the short video platform Vine only pulled in 14 percent of those surveyed.[5] Because our information channels are shifting, publishers are making an effort to meet consumers where they get information. News organizations are going digital, with a presence across all social media.

2

PULLING THE WOOL OVER YOUR EYES

Every year the Oxford Dictionaries select a Word of the Year. In 2013, the word was "selfie," and in 2015 they chose the first ever pictograph—a face with tears of joy emoji. After much debate, the chosen term for 2016 was "post-truth." Other contenders were "alt-right" and "adulting." "Post-truth" was selected because 2016 had been a politically charged year. "Post-truth" is defined as "relating to or denoting circumstances in which objective facts are less influential in shaping public opinion than appeals to emotion and personal belief."[1]

When Pigs Fly

Fake news is a story, whether it is a video or written article that is deliberately false with the intent to deceive. At its lowest level, fake news confuses the reader and is a waste of time. At its highest, fake news can sway elections, spur conspiracy theories, and shape ideologies. As news consumers, it is important to understand the different kinds of content that mislead or misinform.

Fake news is deliberately false, with the intent to deceive its readers. Fake news can sway elections and give rise to conspiracy theories.

Misinformation is incorrect information, but sometimes it is a genuine mistake or a product of sloppy reporting. But it can also intentionally spread false information for a purpose. Disinformation is misinformation with the deliberate intent to deceive. The motive is often to make money, gain power, or cause confusion.

In a *New Yorker* magazine interview, former President Barack Obama expressed concerns about the current mucky state of the media:

An explanation of climate change from a Nobel Prize–winning physicist looks exactly the same on your Facebook page as the denial of climate change by somebody on the Koch brothers' payroll. And the capacity to disseminate misinformation, wild conspiracy theories, to paint the opposition in wildly negative light without any rebuttal—that has accelerated in ways that much more sharply polarize the electorate and make it very difficult to have a common conversation.[2]

Fake news not only agitates political discourse, but also disrupts scientific research and knowledge. Climate change science is a victim of fake news time and time again, especially when new research is presented. For example, when climate researchers published a paper in the scientific journal *Nature Geoscience* in which they discussed the amount of time before humans destroy the climate to the point of no return, they estimated that the tipping point is a bit further out than originally thought. Far-right websites took that real news and ran with it. Fake news stories shamed scientists and how they got it all wrong with regard to global warming.[3]

Good scientific research embraces uncertainty, and seeks to find better solutions and clearer answers. However, the fake headlines exploited uncertainty and turned what is a powerful tool in science into seeds of doubt.

First Coined

Donald Trump claims he invented it. Although he has publically used the term over three hundred times, Trump was not the first to use or tweet the phrase.[4] According to Merriam-Webster, the phrase "fake news" harkens back to early days of baseball and ragtime music. In the late nineteenth century, fake news appeared in newspaper headlines. For example in the *Cincinnati Commercial Tribune* June 7, 1890, issue, a headline read: "Secretary Brunnell Declares Fake News About His People Is Being Telegraphed Over the Country."[5] But fake news has been around longer, it was just called false news then—same meaning, different words.

Fake News Is Not News

Although the term "fake news" has become popular in the last few years, it didn't sprout from the loins of Facebook and Twitter. Bogus news has been around pretty much since the invention of the printing press.

A leading figure of early American history dipped his quill in a steamy pile of forgery. In 1782, Benjamin Franklin made up a false story that was published in a Boston newspaper, the *Independent Chronicle*. His fake letter described a gruesome collaboration between King George and Native Americans to

In 1782, Benjamin Franklin published a false story in a Boston newspaper about King George and Native Americans collecting American scalps.

collect scalps of more than seven hundred innocent American victims. Among the hundreds of farmers' scalps were scalps of women, young boys and girls, and even a "Box of Birch Bark, containing 29 little Infants' Scalps of various Sizes."[6] Both the colonists and the British had employed armies of Native Americans during the fight, but Franklin exaggerated in hopes of swaying British readers in American's favor. The letter was reprinted several times in both London and US newspapers.

About a hundred years later, "yellow journalism" reared its ugly head. Born from two newspaper owners, William Randolph Hearst of the *New York Journal* and Joseph Pulitzer of the *New York World*, yellow journalism of the 1890s used dramatic, exaggerated, and sometimes entirely false stories to help sell newspapers. Each paper would report sensational headlines that would either make readers cry or shake their fists towards the sky.

It got worse during the Spanish-American War. Battling it out over sensational headlines, the *New York World* and *New York Journal* reported horrifying falsehoods about female prisoners, sinking battleships, and starving innocent families—the nastier the better.[7] Although yellow journalism is said to have ended in the twentieth century, scandalous stories still tend to stick, and this is perhaps why fake news is so successful.

Other Fakes

Other terms or phrases that have entered the false media lexicon include "alternative facts," "gaslighting," and "extreme bias."

Alternative facts first popped up on TV news when White House senior counselor Kellyanne Conway was interviewed

Comparisons of the inaugural crowds of Barack Obama (*top*) and Donald Trump (*bottom*) on the National Mall, Washington, DC

on MSNBC. She was fielding questions about why then-White House Press Secretary Sean Spicer exaggerated the size of Trump's inauguration crowd. "This was the largest audience to ever witness an inauguration—period—both in person and around the globe," Spicer told the press.[8] When several media organizations called out the obvious falsehood, Conway said Spicer gave an "alternative fact."[9] Although alternative facts have been paraded around as just a reframing of facts, such as the glass is half full instead of half empty,[10] they are indeed another way to confuse and mislead news consumers.

Gaslighting is another tool of fake news. A psychological manipulation, gaslighting encourages readers to distrust their own reality. The purveyor of gaslighting hopes to wedge a seed of doubt into consumers' minds to make them second-guess what their senses tell them. For example, in the aftermath of the horrific school shooting in Parkland, Florida, the outspoken, concerned teens and citizens protesting for better gun control were rumored to be paid protestors or crisis actors. Fake news circulated in hopes of dismissing their voices of resistance. Photos of grievers were taken out of context and shared on social media. However, the phony idea of paid dissent is not new. The gaslighting technique was used during the civil rights movement to belittle and minimize demands for equality.[11]

Another form of fakery is a story drowning in extreme bias. When all quoted sources are on the same bandwagon, when they all say the same thing or support the same bias angle, you're reading an extreme biased article. An extreme biased story pulls information out of context, or has a slant or angle that is exaggerated. Biased stories often state opinions as straight fact but offer zero evidence to their claims. If the story seems to come from a place of "us against them," then it may have an extreme bias. An example of opinion touted as news is the *Hannity Show* on Fox News. Sean Hannity is a conservative political commentator. A journalist reports the news, whereas a commentator will give opinion of the news.

BEHIND THE BOGUS

Early in the morning on September 11, 2014, residents of St. Mary Parish, Louisiana, woke up to a startling text message. Alerting citizens of an explosion at a local chemical manufacturing plant, the message warned residents of toxic fumes in the area, and cautioned "Take Shelter." It told people to check local media for more information.

The news story spread over Twitter with different accounts documenting the disaster. The hashtag #ColumbianChemicals included images of the chemical plant in flames. Videos taken from a nearby gas stationed showed plumes of black smoke rising in the distance. Messages of the news were sent to local and national journalists and media organizations. One tweet showed CNN's homepage with the news. Another tweet shared a YouTube video of a TV tuned into an Arabic news channel where ISIS had already claimed credit for the explosion.[1]

But the Columbia Chemicals plant doesn't exist. The text messages, photos of smoke and flames, even the videos were all fake. It was all a hoax. A Wikipedia page describing the event even surfaced. But this wasn't just a simple prank put on by some bored loser. It was a highly coordinated and

This Columbian Chemicals plant is in Brazil—and was never on fire in Louisiana, despite text warnings, video, and news reports that said it was.

organized disinformation campaign involving probably a dozen or so people, including programmers and producers. According to one investigative reporter, the headquarters for the mastermind conspiracy was over 5,000 miles (8,046 kilometers) away from US soil.

The Agency of Fake News

New York Times reporter Adrian Chen had already sniffed out suspicious behavior from the Russian organization, the Internet

Research Agency. Located in St. Petersburg, the Internet Research Agency was known for spreading pro-Kremlin propaganda using fake identities.[2] After Chen recognized similarities in the Columbia Chemical hoax, he decided to investigate. Chen flew to Russia and interviewed former employees of the Internet Research Agency. His sources described the organization as industrialized trolling.[3]

This unassuming building was the location of the Internet Research Agency, a troll farm in St. Petersburg, Russia. With a vast budget, these trolls sought to disrupt the 2016 US presidential election.

A troll is someone who deliberately stirs the pot by posting provocative comments on social media or in an online community. For example, a troll will slam malicious comments on a Facebook post, or reply to a tweet with a comment so far off topic it will inject confusion. Trolls heckle debates and attempt to sow discord.

The Internet Research Agency is a troll farm or factory— an organized fleet of trolls who work together to defeat truth and civil discourse. The Agency has hundreds of workers in its convoy. Their mission is to manufacture disinformation on Facebook, Twitter, Instagram, and YouTube using bogus accounts. Chen followed the trail of fake social media accounts and found the same phony players who helped spread the Columbia Chemical fake news.[4]

But this was just the beginning of the Internet Research Agency's information warfare. A few years later, the trolls, with a little bit more experience with the English language and operations, deployed a project aimed at the US 2016 presidential election.

With a budget of millions of dollars, Project Lakhta employed hundreds of people in its online operations, from administrative support to fake news content creators. To hide the Russian activity link, the Agency purchased space on computer servers located in the United States, and used a private network to set up hundreds of fake accounts on social media, such as Facebook, Twitter, and Instagram. The Russian wolves dressed in stars and stripes, pretending to be socially and politically active Americans. Some accounts were completely fictitious, while others involved stolen identities. The hundreds of fake

Troll's Little Cheerleader

If a troll is a person who authors fake news, a bot is the troll's digital cheerleader. A bot is an automated social media account that is programmed to help spread phony news. Social bots play an important role. A bot's job is to share, retweet, and highlight the voices of disinformation. Once a troll has posted a fake story, they will use a fleet of bots to spray the news across the Twitterverse. Like cheerleaders, the bots pump up their audience for fake news. But bots are also used to infuse confusion and distract from the real news.

personas created social media groups to communicate and interact with real Americans. The goal was to insert distrust in both presidential candidates and the political system.[5] But the Agency was the only one interested in meddling with the US election.

Homegrown Operations

Travel five thousand miles southeast from Russia, and you will find the home of another disinformation campaign. However, this one is far less sophisticated and more homegrown. In the small Macedonian town of Veles, a group of teens were looking to make an easy buck. Unethical entrepreneurs, the teens saw an opportunity and exploited it: they launched over 100 pro-Trump websites complete with fake news.

Some stories were plagiarized from right-wing American sites and fitted with new catchy headlines, while other stories were completely fabricated. But every fake news story catered to their target audience—Trump supporters. The teens learned the best way to make money was to use Facebook. When consumers started clicking and sharing, the pennies piled up. The more readers clicked through, the more money they made from ads on their websites. Popular headlines ranged from the imminent criminal indictment of Hillary Clinton to endorsements for Trump from the Pope.[6] The popular stories generated thousands of dollars. The teens didn't care about American politics or who won the 2016 election, they just saw dollar signs—or the Macedonian denar (MKD). One hundred MKDs are equal to about two US dollars. The teens just wanted enough money for new cell phones or watches.

Homegrown fake news doesn't always come from outside the United States. It's a lucrative business, and Paul Horner capitalized on it. Horner was an American writer with a taste for phony stories, making a living from telling fake news. At one point in his career, he even pretended to win a massive Powerball jackpot.[7] Horner's claim to fame was his influence in the US 2016 election. He even bragged during an interview with the *Washington Post*, "I think Trump is in the White House because of me."[8]

His most successful bogus story was posted on a fake ABC News website (that he created). The headline read: "Donald Trump Protester Speaks Out: "I Was Paid $3,500 To Protest

For Donald Trump, "fake news" tends to be any news he doesn't like or news that shows him in a negative light. Negative news is not fake news.

Trump's Rally." It went viral. Even Trump's campaign manager retweeted the story before it was found out to be fake news.[9]

Horner profited from his followers not fact-checking and sharing without concern. While he believed his stories to be satire and not fake news, Horner claimed he was educating people. But his misinformation stories were popular and shared widely, only adding to an already noisy media. In 2017, Horner passed away from an accidental drug overdose, and his fake news empire crumbled in the wake of his death. Some people were unsure if news of his death was just another phony headline.[10]

Whether disinformation or alternative facts, the people behind fake news bank on the consumer to like, share, or retweet without regard for the validity of the story. Fake news stories aim to disrupt, cause confusion, and instill fear. And when those bogus headlines spread, the effects grow nastier and become a lot more than the consumer bargained for.

4

A Few Facts
Short of a Story

"A lie gets halfway around the world before the truth has a chance to get its pants on," said the former British Prime Minister Winston Churchill.[1] Or was it Mark Twain who said it, but it was boots instead of pants? Ironically the poignant and powerful quote has been misattributed to Thomas Jefferson, John Randolph, and even popular fantasy author Terry Pratchett.[2] That quote has traveled across the internet before the truth could get on its pants or boots. While misattribution of a quote from a hundred years ago is mostly innocuous, nowadays incorrectly attributed quotes are the entrails of a fake news story.

House of Cards

The first step in fishing truth from the ocean of lies is to equip yourself with the proper tools. Guard precious brain cells and valuable time, with tips and tricks on how to identify the fakery.

Scrolling through your Facebook feed, you come across a headline claiming that a Greenpeace activist did the unthinkable—the dude tried to hug a shark and got his arm

How can you avoid fake news? Don't limit yourself to a single website—verify sources and know who is responsible for those sources.

bitten off during the forced embrace.[3] Although everyone knows sharks like their space, you're resisting the urge to click the headline and share the stupidity with everyone you know on Facebook, Twitter, and Tumblr. Before clogging up the communication line with rubbish, read beyond the headline. Headlines don't tell the full story and are often phrased in a sensational and exaggerated way to grab attention.

Sometimes a fake headline will take information out of context. Rule of thumb: read past the headline and into the article. If the story continues with a dramatic and inflated style, it is probably fake. Next, check the author. Look for information about the author. Wander over to the "About Us" section. If it is a legitimate news organization, the page will offer a story of the business, such as the history of the news outlet, or a mission statement from the organization's leaders.

Check the story's sources. Who is quoted? Which experts did the reporter bring in to offer insight into the topic? Paul Horner, the man who claimed responsibility for Trump's victory at the polls because of his fake news stories, wrote and published a story titled "Obama Signs Executive Order Banning the Pledge of Allegiance in Schools Nationwide." The headline was juicy and highlighted a popular rumor.[4] However, reading past the headline, the sources quoted are Fappy the Anti-Masturbation Dolphin and Sock it Forward.[5]

Misinformation may use made-up sources, or even bland or generic names. If the sources seem legitimate, then evaluate what they are saying. Do the quotes further the understanding of the issue? Or are they combative and one-sided? If all the

Questions to Ask Fake News

Ask the story three questions to help determine if you're reading fake news or real news.[7]

Where is the story published? Check the URL. Is it a legitimate news website? Beware of common news websites that end with a ".com.co," for example, ABCnews.com.co. These fake news websites are masquerading as real news.[8]

Is the story set in the future? Check the date. Fake news stories can be full of facts, but the facts are distorted or taken out of context or time.

Does the story present both sides of the argument? Or is the story written as *us vs. them*, but the other side is omitted? Fair and accurate reporting offers both sides of the table.

quotes are cheering for the same side, it might be a fake news story or be tilted toward an extreme bias.

Reverse search any images used. A popular image that usually pops up in social media after a flood or hurricane is a shark swimming in the fast lane on a flooded freeway. Images can be altered or doctored to pair with a fake news story. Photos can also be taken completely out of context. Images of the Parkland, Florida, grievers were taken out of context and shared on social media.[6] Right-click on the image and search for it on Google. If the photo pops up in several different stories but the only common theme is the image, then it may be fake news. You can't always believe what you see, or see what you believe.

Finally, consult the experts. If after reading beyond the headline and checking the sources, author, and images, you're still unsure if the story is bogus, seek council from fact-checking experts. Even though the internet has made the creation and spread of fake news more ubiquitous, it has also provided space for investigators of truth and spotters of obfuscation.

Information overload—attention is currency, and misinformation builds fast, with click-throughs, likes, shares, and retweets. Think before you share—be sure the content is legit!

Some good resources are Factcheck.org, snopes.com, and PolitiFact.com.

Spread Like Wildfire

Why do lies travel quicker and farther than truth? We are experiencing an information overload. From hilarious cat videos to the latest political debacle, true or false stories are blasted all over our newsfeed. We can realistically only digest a small portion of the information. Because there is so much junk chumming the waters, it is challenging for real news to surface. A story doesn't have to be true or even be of quality to survive and thrive online. It just has to hold our attention.

The attention economy explains the demand and supply of information generated and consumed in the grand marketplace of ideas, especially on social media.[9] Author and academic Thomas Davenport defines attention as "focused mental engagement on a particular item of information. Items come into our awareness, we attend to a particular item, and then we decide whether to act."[10]

Attention is currency. Every click-through, like, share, or retweet is like scoring points. With 2.13 billion monthly active users on Facebook,[11] misinformation builds momentum quickly and reaches many readers in little time. Information, fake or not, is also used as a social currency in the attention economy. Being the first to share breaking news, regardless of its validity, is used to build relationships or status within networks or groups. And because we tend to surround ourselves with people who share our views or who are like-minded, fake news gets passed around.The more it's shared, the more value it attains in the attention economy.

Plus, we all love a good rumor. A 2018 study examined the flow of rumors on Twitter and found that from 2006 to 2017, approximately 3 million people spread almost 126,000 rumors.[12] Note it was real people, not bots, that shared the fake news. Rumors that spread are ones that tend to play on our fears and emotions. But it is the simple rumors that are inclined to stick.[13]

For example, evaluate the buzz that the average person swallows eight spiders per year. Lisa Holst, a journalist, was irritated by our tendency to believe just about anything on the internet. So she pulled the fake spider fact from a 1954 book on insect folklore, along with other ridiculous factoids she made up, and published them in a story about the gullibility of modern society. Ironically, the bogus statistic stuck while her story to prove how easily rumors spread did not. The spider swallowing rumor is one the most popular fake facts out there.[14]

Circulate the Agenda

Fake news can make a person shake their head and chuckle in disbelief, while satire can painfully pinch a nerve. Both may highlight sensational activities of politicians and are full of fakery, but the main difference between satire and misinformation is intent.

Satire has been around for a long time. Jonathan Swift's *A Modest Proposal For preventing the Children of Poor People From being a Burthen to Their Parents or Country, and For making them Beneficial to the Publick* (published 1729) was

Satire is not fake news. Satire exists to entertain, whereas fake news's intent is to mislead, misinform, and persuade the consumer toward a specific opinion.

a satirical proposition of a solution for Ireland's poverty. The proposal suggested butchering children of the Irish poor and selling the flesh as food for the wealthy. Swift's satire argued that his solution killed two birds with one stone—solving overpopulation while giving poor families a little extra cash on the side from the sale of their starving kiddos. Swift even offered recipes in his proposal.

Satire is meant to be funny, even if grotesque like Swift's proposal. But the main purpose or motive behind the funny and strange stories is to poke fun at government, society, or leaders of political corruption. Modern examples of satire in news are the *Onion* or the *New Yorker's* "The Borowitz Report."[15] Usually satire is labeled as such, but consumers may have to search for the label.

While satire has the intent to call out foibles, fake news has a different agenda. Misinformation is not labeled and is created in the image of real news. Its intent is to mislead, misinform, and persuade the consumer towards a specific opinion. Satire may evoke laughter, whereas fake news can summon fear. Or sometimes the agenda of fake news is simply to be the loudest voice in the room.

GETTING THE WRONG END OF THE STICK

Remember the photo of the shark swimming on the freeway? Even though the image has been debunked, it continues to resurface during massive storms or in the aftermath of severe weather hurricanes. The shark has managed to make an appearance on the freeways of Texas, Puerto Rico, and Florida. In Australia, the shark was named Cindy—she followed a fisherman after he freed her from a net. In 2012, the shark showed up at the bottom of an escalator at a shopping mall in Kuwait.[1]

While the image is silly fakery, the shark distracts from the true coverage of real people suffering in the aftermath of a natural disaster. Fake news can't be shoved under the rug and forgotten. When fake news is not critically evaluated, the ideas or ideologies can stick around and continue to cause disruption and destruction in our communication lines.

Remember and Reflect

Although the exact origin of the anti-Semitic literature is unknown, *Protocols of the Elders of Zion* (often known as

Some fakes are easier to spot than others, but some tend to linger, even after they're debunked. People love sensational ideas.

Protocols) was first published in 1905 as an appendix to *The Great in the Small: The Coming of the Anti-Christ and the Rule of Satan on Earth* by Russian writer Sergei Nilus. Completely made up and fake, *Protocols* claims to be notes taken from a secret meeting with Jewish leaders. The fabricated script portrays Jews as conspirators with a covert plan to take over the world by controlling the media, economy, and igniting religious contention.

By 1920, *Protocols* had been translated and distributed in Europe, Russia, South America, Japan, and the United

States. The anti-Semitic fake news even made it into the hands of German chancellor Adolf Hitler. It became an important tool used in Nazi propaganda, and twenty-three editions were published. The hateful and completely fake title is still prevalent today. *Protocols* encourages a hateful ideology that still exists today and causes much violence and hate worldwide. Hate groups in the United States and Europe distribute the propaganda to fuel anti-Semitism.[2] According to a 2017 Anti-Defamation League Report, there was a 60 percent surge of anti-Semitic incidents, including vandalism, physical assaults, and attacks on Jewish institutions.[3]

Another falsehood that was birthed many moons ago, but still exists today and is gaining traction, is the conspiracy that the 1969 Apollo moon landing was a hoax. A 2004 poll revealed that 27 percent of Americans between 18 and 24 years old expressed doubts about the moon landing.[4] The question of whether a mission actually made it to the moon has long been a trending topic for conspiracy theorists and fake news creators, with doctored pictures and video footage supporting the bogus claims. In November of 2017, Fox News tweeted an image that encouraged the viewer to be skeptical of the landing.[5]

The hoax about the hoax has oozed into another conspiracy—the flat Earth theory. Flat Earthers, as they are called, believe Earth to be flat and with an edge that continues indefinitely. They also think the moon landing was faked. The Flat Earth Society thinks astronauts have been bribed or coerced into their testimonies, and believe the photographic evidence from NASA cannot be trusted.[6] With celebrity endorsements,

In 1969, the United States absolutely landed men on the moon, but a significant portion of the American people think it was a hoax.

interest in the theory has surged over the past few years and it's trending on Google. This falsehood wedges skepticism into the value and truth of science.

Muddy Waters

Just a few days before the 2016 US presidential election, a story began circulating on Reddit about a complex and detailed conspiracy of emails from Hillary Clinton's presidential campaign chair John Podesta that exposed a secret society of pedophiles operating through a Washington, DC, pizza restaurant. The story claimed that the pizzeria was a popular hangout spot for the Clinton campaign staff. Allegedly, the walls of the joint were covered with creepy sex-themed murals and graffiti, and in the basement was a child sex-slave operation. Supplementing the trending story were photos of the imprisoned children and a map showing underground tunnels linking the pizzeria to other participating businesses.[7]

One man read the story and decided he needed to organize and execute a rescue mission. Armed with an AR-15 semiautomatic rifle, a .38 handgun, and a knife, 28-year old Edgar Maddison Welch burst into the restaurant to save the children. He marched to the back of the pizzeria expecting to find captive children locked in a basement. All he found were cooking supplies.[8] The business didn't even have a basement.

Luckily no one was harmed, and Welch was arrested. His vigilante justice was an epic fail because he failed to fact-check. The story was an elaborate fake, but he was sentenced to four years in jail. The Pizzagate conspiracy managed to saturate social media, went viral on Reddit, and then blasted

Edgar Maddison Welch, who was motivated by fake news about kidnapping and child sex slaves, surrenders to police after having burst into Comet Pizza with a gun.

its way to Twitter, generating thousands of tweets supporting the story.

Pizzagate is just one example of the consequences of fake news. Although it is unclear if the onslaught of fake news swayed the 2016 election, it definitely muddled Americans' heads and polarized the country.[9] After the controversial election, a Gallup poll revealed 77 percent of Americans perceive the nation as politically divided, a record high.[10]

Fake news uses the powerful platform of social media to sow discord and divide the political debate. Trolls and bots promote division over dialogue on already contentious issues, such as race, immigration, religion, and class. People argue about the reality of the world, what is real news, and what is fake news. The divide has seeped into other areas of public discourse, such as action taken to prevent climate change or mass school shootings.[11]

Not All That Glitters Is Gold

According to Gallup's polling history of trust and media, trust in media hit its highest point of 72 percent in 1976 after the successes of investigative journalism of the Watergate scandal.[14] However, a 2016 survey said trust in mass media has dropped to all-time low. At the lowest level in Gallup's polling history, only 32 percent of Americans have a fair amount of trust in the media, such as newspapers, TV, and radio news.

The most significant finding was that only 14 percent of Republicans trust the media, dropping 32 percent from the previous year. Gallup researchers speculate that trust dropped

Fake Panic

Misinformation wreaked havoc in the aftermath of Hurricane Harvey in Texas, only adding to the devastation. Harvey caused $125 billion in damages, ranking number two in most costly hurricanes, second only to Katrina.[12] While residents were trying to pick up the pieces of their lives, fake news shared on social media sparked unnecessary panic. Rumors spread that the city was going to shut off water and electricity. Concerned citizens flooded emergency phone lines. Instead of focusing on the people who truly needed help, emergency operators were tied up battling the fake news. Local police officials asked the public to leave the emergency lines open for active rescue and recovery efforts, and to only share information from local media and officials.[13]

Fake news complicated rescue and recovery efforts in Texas after Hurricane Harvey. Police lines were overwhelmed with questions about power and water being shut off, when no such thing was planned.

because of the repeated rhetoric by conservative pundits saying that Hillary Clinton received more positive media attention, while Donald Trump received negative and unfair coverage.

A 2017 Knight Foundation Survey on Trust, Media, and Democracy followed up with Americans' relationship with the media. Of the 19,000 people surveyed, most (8 out of 10) believed news media is critical to democracy, but they say media is not doing a good job at keeping citizens informed and holding leaders accountable for their actions.[15]

CALLING THEIR BLUFF

Although Donald Trump is fond of blasting the term across Twitter, fake news won't go away by repeating the phrase. Now that we know its scent and recognize the consequences of letting it roam, it's time to combat the beast of misinformation and champion the real news.

Remote Control

The media is a powerful and influential source of information, education, and entertainment. If consumers aren't mindful of their consumption, fake news can creep in and rot their brains. But people need to own their part. The remote is in your hand, the mouse just a click away from closing the browser. Be aware of the algorithms on social media that curate news based on clicks, likes, or shares. Don't passively consume information.

Think of news consumption like the food and beverages we consume daily. Although it tastes good and is fun to eat, a diet full of fat and sugar is unhealthy. Daily digestion of fake news can take a toll on a person's emotional and intellectual being. Instead of a gluttonous consumption of scrolling, clicking, and sharing, put the phone away or close the computer. Practice a mindful media diet.

Be mindful of the media you consume. Set your phone aside for a while, walk away from the noise, disengage, and breathe.

Takes Two to Tango

It can be challenging to navigate the twenty-four-hour news cycle. To survive the noise, sometimes we will disengage, throw our hands up, and walk away from the noise. Or we may block out the noise that is most bothersome—usually ideas, voices, and perspectives different from our own.[1]

Trump resorts to finger-pointing and name-calling when he disagrees with views reported in the media. When Trump talks about fake news, he means something else entirely. Instead of fabricated content, Trump uses the term to describe news coverage that is unsympathetic to his administration and his performance, even when the news reports are accurate. This bias can cause polarization and obstruct civil discourse.

Everyone has biases. Plainly put, bias is defined as singling out or distinguishing one thing from another. People use bias to make decisions every day, such as choosing a bag of baby carrots over a bag of cheesy puffs. But biases can also be negative and directed towards an individual or group of people. A biased attitude is shown when a person assumes superiority over someone else, like saying their news source is better than the other guy's. Some biases are reinforced or learned from family and friends. Because fake news has run rampant across communication lines, a bit of cynicism may surface when trying to figure out whom to believe and whom to distrust. A person may only go to news sources that validate what they already know—to only read news that represents their views.

A confirmation bias is when a person selectively chooses news sources that confirm their beliefs or ideas and opinions and rejects sources that conflict with or contradict their ideas. Bias can seriously damage and limit life experiences, especially if it keeps people in their own little bubble—never stretching their minds or knowledge. Fake news feeds on biases. Keep information channels open. Read a story from a news source that you don't typically read. If you're a diehard Fox News

Change the channel every now and then. If you're a diehard fan of one channel, flip to another to see if it's confirming what you've already heard.

fan, flip the channel to MSNBC. Challenge your biases. You can read more about how to do this in another book in this series, *The Bubble of Confirmation Bias.*

But news consumers are not the only ones with biases. News sources tend to also fall somewhere along a political spectrum. Although it is the media's responsibility to be fair and accurate, some news organizations tend to favor certain stories, sources, or headlines. To check for bias in news media, ask a few questions: [2]

Does the story lack diversity? News media should have reporters, sources, and experts that represent the diversity of the community it serves, including gender and race diversity.

Is the story missing a voice? A biased story may omit voices that oppose their view. To show an unbiased view, a news story should offer both sides to the story.[3]

Is the language loaded? Biased media stories will use loaded terminology to help sway the reader to their side, such as labeling someone as a "terrorist." But biased language can also be subtle. For example, using words that hold a certain connotation, like selecting "suspension" instead of "withdraw." The meaning of a sentence can completely change by manipulating a single word.[4]

Whether bias comes from an individual or the media, hold both accountable. Challenge assumptions. There is a strong connection between tolerance, compassion, and being aware of biases. Strengthen democracy and fight fake news by acknowledging different perspectives and move to a platform for dialogue instead of a podium for biases.

Bottom Line

Craft personal goals for consuming media, and check if those goals are being met by the content consumed. If goals aren't being met, don't put your head in the sand or whine about the glut of phony media. Instead, evaluate your news habits. Seek news outside of social media. Read editorials of major and local newspapers to gather a sense of both sides of an issue. Distribute and share only confirmed and factual media messages and stories.

Against the Law

A new law in Germany is attempting to tackle fake news on social media. Starting in 2018, Germany enforced a law that requires Facebook, Twitter, YouTube, and other social media sites to quickly take down and remove hate speech, fake news, and illegal material. If a social platform doesn't comply within twenty-four hours of being notified, the company can be fined up to fifty million euros.[5] The European Union is also navigating legislature against fake news. But they're taking it slow. Some governments are weary about infringing on free speech. Other EU officials hope social media companies will step up to stop the spread of misinformation.[6]

Advocate for change. If you read a story with obvious falsehoods, contact the source and let them know. Hold news sources accountable, but in a respectful and well-researched manner. Define misinformation and point to accurate sources. A clearly supported message will go a lot further than simply name-calling. If the news organization is after truthful reporting, it will likely retract or correct the story.

Call or write media outlets when you see forms of biased reporting, for example a panel of all-white, straight cisgender males discussing issues that affect LGBTQ people

How can you help fight fake news? Hold news sources accountable, but in a respectful and well-researched manner. Define misinformation and point to accurate sources.

of color. Demand fair and accurate reporting from the news organizations that claim to be already doing it.

And don't forget to take a good, long look in the mirror and spot those biases. Critically evaluate assumptions and trace them back to their birthplace.

No News Is Not Good News

In the modern world, interacting with artificial intelligence is sometimes an everyday experience. Snapchat's face effects or Instagram's filters are examples of ways in which users manipulate reality using artificial intelligence. But what if that technology was used against news consumers? What if videos popped up on your social media feed showing Hillary Clinton in the basement of a pizzeria tormenting stolen children? This is the future of fake news. "Seeing is believing" is becoming a thing of ancient past. In the ecosystem of fakery, consumers will have to hold skepticism close.

Sleight of Hand

A new breed of counterfeit has entered the family of fake news—face-morphing technology. While Photoshop has been used to doctor still images, like the shark swimming on the freeway, new technology can manipulate video footage.

Software developed at Stanford University, Face2Face is a real-time facial reenactment manipulation tool. The software allows a person to literally turn a frown upside-down.

Researchers captured live video of a person's facial expressions with a webcam and downloaded video clips from YouTube to manipulate. They demonstrated their puppeteering technology using videos of George W. Bush, Vladimir Putin, and Donald Trump.[1] The results were uncanny.

Using YouTube videos, the morphing technology studies and gathers mouth pattern data, frame-by-frame. Then, using a basic webcam, facial-tracking technology drives the animation in the video. Watch as a person in front of a webcam scrunches

The future of fake news may involve face-morphing technology, where one person can be made to look and sound like another.

up his lips or opens his mouth in a wide yawn, while Putin mimics his moves in real time. The motion capture records a person's facial expression with a webcam and renders those movements as the video plays out in real time.[2]

Researchers say short videos make it harder to retrieve the person-specific mouth behavior. Or when the subject has too much facial hair, it can be tricky. While the developers hope the technology can be used in teleconferencing or on-the-fly dubbing of videos with translated audio, the tool could fall into the wrong hands. Making a former US president smirk or frown is one thing, but this is just the beginning.

Smoke and Mirrors

Also called voice transformation or voice conversion, voice morphing is a technology that modifies and clones a person's speech pattern to create an original speech as if spoken by the target speaker.[3] The technology can be used for dubbing movies or TV shows. The military has even thought to use it as a psychological weapon.

Created in the Los Alamos National Laboratory in New Mexico, voice-morphing technology was initially developed after Iraq's invasion of Kuwait in 1990.[4] Pentagon planners speculated using the technology for PSYOPS, or psychological operations. According to the official Pentagon policy, "PSYOPS" are "planned operations to convey selected information and indicators to foreign audiences to influence their emotions, motives, objective reasoning, and ultimately the behavior of foreign governments, organizations, groups, and individuals."[5]

Reality of Virtual Reality

With so much information and news competing in the attention economy, news organizations are exploring ways to engage and connect with audiences. Virtual reality journalism aims at building participants' empathy for turmoil outside their own backyard.[9] The *New York Times* award-winning virtual reality project "The Displaced" offers a glimpse into the lives affected by war and persecution. Nearly 60 million people, including 30 million children, are displaced from their homes by war in countries like Syria, Afghanistan, and Nigeria. The multimedia project tells the story of three children through photo essays, 360-degree- view videos, and interviews. The powerful experience shows war through the eyes of young refugees.

Covert operators played around with the idea of using voice morphing to forge audiotapes of Saddam Hussein saying inappropriate things and blanket the fake news across Iraq and the Arab world. But the plan was nixed because of skepticism over the technology. Plus Arab coalition partners raised concerns over using the new tool.[6]

Another example of audiovisual magic comes from the University of Washington. Researchers created a tool that converts audio files into realistic mouth movements and then layers the mouth movements onto a video. Using former president Barack Obama, researchers took audio footage

Virtual reality journalism is on the rise, with viewers able to witness realities other than their own. Walking a mile in another person's shoes lends a personal angle to stories.

from different interviews over the years and grafted them on to a present-day Obama. The process was not easy and did take time. They needed seventeen hours of footage to gather the data and mimic his mouth movements.[7]

The lip-syncing technology can only use actual speech from the target and not fabricated speech. But other software is playing with the idea of manipulating audio recordings to put words into someone's mouth. Adobe's Project Voco is essentially the Photoshop for audio files. The software needs only about twenty minutes of a person's speech to edit a digitized recording in seconds. In a live demo, Adobe took a recording of a man saying, "I kissed my dogs and my wife" and changed it to "I kissed Jordan three times."[8] Creators say the software would make voiceovers, dialogue, and narration easier to edit, instead of having to re-record or hire voiceover actors. But it also presents a deluge of opportunities for fake news creators. Project Voco has not been released to the public, and creators are taking note of possible misapplications.

Call the Shots

The future immersive platforms in journalism are both exciting and terrifying. While projects like "The Displaced" may have the power to motivate action for change, fake news stories may also have the power of persuasion. Misinformation is being weaponized for power, profit, or to distract. Fake news or the accusations of fake news is pushing out the ethical and accurate stories from our communication lines. How will the public defend truth in the onslaught of disinformation?

Twitter has over 300 million monthly active users, and nearly 48 million of those accounts are thought to be bots.[10] Two students studying computer science at UC Berkeley decided to launch a counterattack against them. Becoming part of the solution instead of feeding the beast, Ash Bhat and Rohan Phadte built a bot-busting weapon to be used on the political battlefield of Twitter. The duo was tired of the fake accounts dragging the political discourse through the mud.

Their Google Chrome browser extension inserts a button onto Twitter profiles that prompts the user to "Botcheck.me."

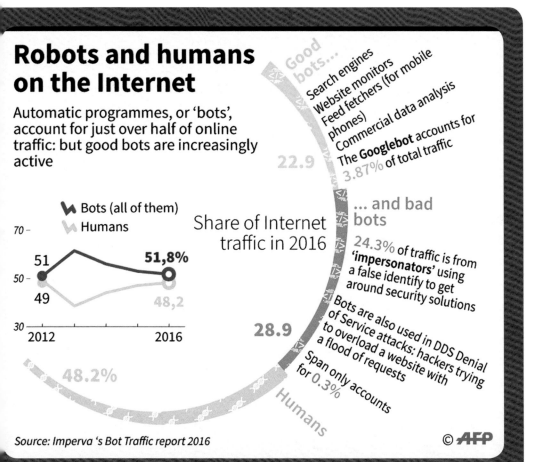

Robots and humans on the Internet

Automatic programmes, or 'bots', account for just over half of online traffic: but good bots are increasingly active

Good bots...

Search engines
Website monitors
Feed fetchers (for mobile phones)
Commercial data analysis

The **Googlebot** accounts for 3.87% of total traffic

22.9

Bots (all of them)
Humans

70 –

Share of Internet traffic in 2016

51
50 –
51,8%
49
48,2

30
2012   2016

48.2%

... and bad bots

24.3% of traffic is from 'impersonators' using a false identify to get around security solutions

Bots are also used in DDS Denial of Service attacks: hackers trying to overload a website with a flood of requests Span only accounts for 0.3%

28.9

Humans

Source: Imperva 's Bot Traffic report 2016   © **AFP**

How to spot a bot? It can be tricky, but not all bots are bad! Still, if something seems suspicious, it may be. Explore, verify, and think about the media you consume and where it comes from.

Once it's clicked, the user gets a diagnosis of whether the account is controlled by a person or an automated bot. The check is right about nine times out of ten.[11] They aren't alone in the fight. Other bot-hunting tools are available, such as Botometer, a program created by Indiana University computer scientists that checks the activity of a Twitter account and gives it a score based on how likely it is to be bot.[12]

You call the shots. Become critical media consumers, and ethical and honest storytellers. Weed out inaccuracies. Be the upstander who corrects misinformation. Don't be the bully shoving real news in the corner. A defender of investigative journalism and journalism standards, editor Monica Almeida describes her experience reporting in Ecuador, where press freedom is under attack:

...Since then I have written many stories, about everything from violent events to white-collar crime. Each one has been a great responsibility and a big challenge. It is not only about being accurate and pursuing the truth; it also is about using words with a purpose. Sometimes that purpose is to give people better information so they can make better choices, sometimes it is to provoke a change in a specific situation, or to defend fundamental liberties, or to stand up for someone or something. Sometimes it is also a matter of not following the agenda set by the powerful, but of telling the stories of people affected by that agenda.[13]

CHAPTER NOTES

Chapter 1
In the Newsroom

1. "Who, What, When, Where, Why, and How," *Columbia Journalism Review*, September 2013, https://archives.cjr.org/cover_story/who_what_when.php.
2. Delbert Tran, "The Fourth Estate as the Final Check," *Media Freedom and Information Access Clinic*, November 22, 2016, https://law.yale.edu/mfia/case-disclosed/fourth-estate-final-check.
3. "The Universal News Drivers," *Stony Book Center for News Literacy*, http://drc.centerfornewsliteracy.org/content/universal-news-drivers.
4. Christopher B. Daly, "How Woodrow Wilson's Propaganda Machine Changed American Journalism," *Smithsonian*, April 28, 2017, https://www.smithsonianmag.com/history/how-woodrow-wilsons-propaganda-machine-changed-american-journalism-180963082/.
5. Jeffrey Gottfried and Elisa Shearer, "News Use Across Social Media Platforms 2016," Pew Research Center, May 26, 2016, http://www.journalism.org/2016/05/26/news-use-across-social-media-platforms-2016/.

Chapter 2
Pulling the Wool Over Your Eyes

1. "Word of the Year 2016 is...," English Oxford Dictionaries, https://en.oxforddictionaries.com/word-of-the-year/word-of-the-year-2016.

2. David Remnick, "Obama Reckons with a Trump Presidency," November 28, 2016, *New Yorker*, https://www.newyorker.com/magazine/2016/11/28/obama-reckons-with-a-trump-presidency?mbid=social_twitter.

3. Michael Grubb, "We're Climate Researchers and Our Work Was Turned into Fake News," *The Conversation*, January 25, 2018, https://theconversation.com/were-climate-researchers-and-our-work-was-turned-into-fake-news-89999.

4. Callum Borchers, "Trump Falsely Claims Again That He Coined the Term 'Fake News,'" *Washington Post*, October 26, 2017, https://www.washingtonpost.com/news/the-fix/wp/2017/10/26/trump-falsely-claims-again-that-he-coined-the-term-fake-news/?utm_term=.1cf08e59c655.

5. Merriam-Webster, "The Real Story of 'Fake News,'" https://www.merriam-webster.com/words-at-play/the-real-story-of-fake-news.

6. Benjamin Franklin, "Supplement to the Boston Independent Chronicle," 1782, https://founders.archives.gov/documents/Franklin/01-37-02-0132#BNFN-01-37-02-0132-fn-0001.

7. PBS, "Yellow Journalism," Crucible of the Empire, http://www.pbs.org/crucible/frames/_journalism.html.

8. Lori Robertson and Robert Farley, "Fact Check: The Controversy Over Trump's Inauguration Crowd Size," *USA Today,* January 24, 2017, https://www.usatoday.com/story/

news/politics/2017/01/24/fact-check-inauguration-crowd-size/96984496/.

9. Rebecca Sinderbrand, "How Kellyanne Conway Ushered in the Era of 'Alternative Facts,'" *Washington Post*, January 22, 2017, https://www.washingtonpost.com/news/the-fix/wp/2017/01/22/how-kellyanne-conway-ushered-in-the-era-of-alternative-facts/.

10. Olivia Nuzzi, "Kellyanne Conway Is a Star: Not Your Star, Perhaps. But That's the Point," *New York Media*, March 18, 2017, http://nymag.com/daily/intelligencer/2017/03/kellyanne-conway-trumps-first-lady.html.

11. Niraj Chokshifeb, "Crisis Actor' Isn't a New Smear. The Idea Goes Back to the Civil War Era," *New York Times*, February 24, 2018, https://www.nytimes.com/2018/02/24/us/crisis-actors-florida-shooting.html?smid=fb-share.

Chapter 3

Behind the Bogus

1. Jeffery Brown, "Why Are Russian Trolls Spreading Online Hoaxes in the U.S.?" *PBS NewsHour*, June 8, 2015, https://www.pbs.org/newshour/show/why-are-russian-trolls-spreading-online-hoaxes-in-the-u-s.

2. Shaun Walker, "The Russian Troll Factory at the Heart of the Meddling Allegations," *The Guardian*, April 2, 2015, https://www.theguardian.com/world/2015/apr/02/putin-kremlin-inside-russian-troll-house.

3. Adrian Chen, "The Agency" *New York Times Magazine*, June 2, 2015, https://www.nytimes.com/2015/06/07/magazine/the-agency.html.

4. Ibid.

5. "Watch Rosenstein's Full Announcement of the Indictment of 13 Russians," *Washington Post*, February 16, 2018 https://www.youtube.com/watch?v=hlGm5tse8ek.

6. Craig Silverman and Lawrence Alexander, "How Teens in the Balkans Are Duping Trump Supporters with Fake News," *Buzzfeed*, November 3, 2016, https://www.buzzfeed.com/craigsilverman/how-macedonia-became-a-global-hub-for-pro-trump-misinfo?utm_term=.syZ4NBMraz#.psLpGM51bx).

7. Abby Ohlheiser, "Who Do You Believe When a Famous Internet Hoaxer Is Said to Be Dead?" *Washington Post*, September 27, 2017, https://www.washingtonpost.com/news/the-intersect/wp/2017/09/27/who-do-you-believe-when-a-famous-internet-hoaxer-is-said-to-be-dead/?utm_term=.dfa14494cec5.

8. Laurel Wamsley, "Paul Horner, Fake News Purveyor Who Claimed Credit for Trump's Win, Found Dead at 38," NPR, September 27, 2017, https://www.npr.org/sections/thetwo-way/2017/09/27/554050916/paul-horner-fake-news-purveyor-who-claimed-credit-for-trump-s-win-found-dead-at-.

9. Louis Jacobson, "No, Someone Wasn't Paid $3,500 to Protest Donald Trump; It's Fake News," *PolitiFact*, November 17th, 2016, http://www.politifact.com/truth-o-meter/statements/2016/nov/17/blog-posting/no-someone-wasnt-paid-3500-protest-donald-trump-it/.

10. Daniel Funke, "Weeks After His Death, Most of Paul Horner's Fake News Sites Are Down. So What's Left?" Poynter, November 7, 2017, https://www.poynter.org/news/weeks-after-his-death-most-paul-horners-fake-news-sites-are-down-so-whats-left.

Chapter 4
A Few Facts Short of a Story

1. Joshua Gillin, "NFL's Colin Kaepernick Incorrectly Credits Winston Churchill for Quote About Lies," PolitiFact, October 9th, 2017, http://www.politifact.com/punditfact/statements/2017/oct/09/colin-kaepernick/nfls-colin-kaepernick-incorrectly-credits-winston-/.

2. "A Lie Can Travel Halfway Around the World While the Truth Is Putting on Its Shoes," Quote Investigator, July 13, 2014, https://quoteinvestigator.com/2014/07/13/truth/.

3. "Did a Greenpeace Activist Get His Arm Bitten Off After Hugging a White Shark?" Snopes.com, February 1, 2018, https://www.snopes.com/fact-check/greenpeace-activist-get-arm-bitten-off-hugging-white-shark/.

4. "Executive Disorder," Snopes.com, August 16, 2016, https://www.snopes.com/fact-check/pledge-of-allegiance-ban/.

5. Caroline Wallace, "Obama Did Not Ban the Pledge," FactCheck, September 2, 2016, https://www.factcheck.org/2016/09/obama-did-not-ban-the-pledge/.

6. "Is Laura Phelps a Crisis Actor Who Lost a Child at Both Sandy Hook and Marjory Stoneman Douglas?" Snopes.com, https://www.snopes.com/fact-check/is-laura-phelps-a-crisis-actor-who-lost-a-child-at-both-sandy-hook-and-parkland/.

7. Nick Robins-Early, "How to Recognize a Fake News Story," Huffington Post, November 27, 2016, https://www.huffingtonpost.com/entry/fake-news-guide-facebook_us_5831c6aae4b058ce7aaba169?section=politics.

8. Elle Hunt, "What Is Fake News? How to Spot It and What You Can Do to Stop It," Guardian, December 17, 2016, https://

www.theguardian.com/media/2016/dec/18/what-is-fake-news-pizzagate.

9.   Giovanni Luca Ciampaglia, et al., "The Production of Information in the Attention Economy," *Scientific Reports*, May 19, 2015, https://www.nature.com/articles/srep09452.

10. Thomas H. Davenport and John C. Beck, "The Attention Economy: Understanding the New Currency of Business," Harvard Business Press, 2002.

11. Facebook News Room, https://newsroom.fb.com/company-info/.

12. Peter Dizikes, "Study: On Twitter, False News Travels Faster Than True Stories," *MIT News*, March 8, 2018, http://news.mit.edu/2018/study-twitter-false-news-travels-faster-true-stories-0308.

13. Taylor Clark, "The 8½ Laws of Rumor Spread," *Psychology Today*, June 9, 2016, https://www.psychologytoday.com/us/articles/200811/the-8-laws-rumor-spread.

14. "Does the Average Person Swallow Eight Spiders Per Year?" Snopes.com, April 28, 2014, https://www.snopes.com/fact-check/spiders-inside-her/.

15. "Real vs. Fake News: Detecting Lies, Hoaxes and Clickbait," Columbia College, February 13, 2018, https://columbiacollege-ca.libguides.com/fake_news/satire.

Chapter 5

Getting the Wrong End of the Stick

1.   Brian Koerber, "That Fake Photo of a Shark on a Flooded Highway Has an Even Better Backstory," Mashable, September 14, 2017, https://mashable.com/2017/09/14/shark-on-flooded-highway-hoax-history/#E1SOt.RQ.aqn.

2. "Protocols of the Elders of Zion," United States Holocaust Memorial Museum, https://www.ushmm.org/wlc/en/article.php?ModuleId=10007058.

3. "Anti-Semitic Incidents Surged Nearly 60% in 2017, According to New ADL Report," ADL, February 27, 2018, https://www.adl.org/news/press-releases/anti-semitic-incidents-surged-nearly-60-in-2017-according-to-new-adl-report.

4. "Why Do People Persist in Denying the Moon Landings?" Smithsonian National Air and Space Museum, April 1, 2010, https://airandspace.si.edu/stories/editorial/why-do-people-persist-denying-moon-landings.

5. Robinson Meyer, "In a Tweet, Fox News Seems to Question the Moon Landing," *The Atlantic*, November 20, 2017, https://www.theatlantic.com/science/archive/2017/11/in-a-tweet-fox-news-seems-to-question-the-moon-landing/546431/.

6. The Flat Earth Society, FAQ, https://theflatearthsociety.org/home/index.php/about-the-society/faq.

7. "Chuck E. Sleaze," Snopes.com, https://www.snopes.com/fact-check/pizzagate-conspiracy/.

8. Amanda Robb, "Anatomy of a Fake News Scandal," *Rolling Stone*, November 16, 2017, https://www.rollingstone.com/politics/news/pizzagate-anatomy-of-a-fake-news-scandal-w511904.

9. Brendan Nyhan, "Fake News and Bots May Be Worrisome, but Their Political Power Is Overblown," *New York Times*, February 13, 2018, https://www.nytimes.com/2018/02/13/upshot/fake-news-and-bots-may-be-worrisome-but-their-political-power-is-overblown.html.

10. "Record-High 77% of Americans Perceive Nation as Divided," Gallup News, November 21, 2016, http://news.gallup.com/

poll/197828/record-high-americans-perceive-nation-divided. aspx.

11. Livia Gershon, "Just How Divided Are Americans Since Trump's Election?" History Channel, November 8, 2017, https:// www.history.com/news/just-how-divided-are-americans-since-trumps-election.

12. "Costliest U.S. Tropical Cyclones Tables Updated," National Hurricane Center, January 26, 2018, https://www.nhc.noaa. gov/news/UpdatedCostliest.pdf.

13. Miles O'Brien, "Fake News Reports Are Hindering the Emergency Response to Harvey." PBS NewsHour, August 30, 2017, https://www.pbs.org/newshour/nation/fake-news-reports-hindering-emergency-response-harvey.

14. Art Swift, "Americans' Trust in Mass Media Sinks to New Low," Gallup News, September 14, 2016, http://news.gallup.com/ poll/195542/americans-trust-mass-media-sinks-new-low.aspx.

15. "American Views: Trust, Media And Democracy," Knight Foundation, January 15, 2018, https://knightfoundation.org/ reports/american-views-trust-media-and-democracy.

Chapter 6
Calling Their Bluff

1. "Polarization Is Destroying Us. Let's Fix This," AllSides, https:// www.allsides.com/how-allsides-changes-the-world.

2. "How to Detect Bias in News Media," FAIR, https://fair.org/ take-action-now/media-activism-kit/how-to-detect-bias-in-news-media/.

3. "Detecting Bias in the Media," https://www.edu.gov.mb.ca/ k12/cur/socstud/foundation_gr9/blms/9-1-3g.pdf.

4. "Word Choice Buffer: All You Can Eat. News Biased Explored," University of Michigan, http://umich.edu/~newsbias/wordchoice.html.
5. "Germany Starts Enforcing Hate Speech Law," BBC News, January 1, 2018, http://www.bbc.com/news/technology-42510868.
6. Anya Schiffrin, "How Europe Fights Fake News," *Columbia Journalism Review*, October 26, 2017, https://www.cjr.org/watchdog/europe-fights-fake-news-facebook-twitter-google.php.

Chapter 7
No News Is Not Good News

1. Justus Thies, et al., "Face2Face: Real-time Face Capture and Reenactment of RGB Videos," Stanford University, https://web.stanford.edu/~zollhoef/papers/CVPR2016_Face2Face/paper.pdf.
2. Ibid.
3. Bill Arkin, "When Seeing and Hearing Isn't Believing," *Washington Post*, February 1, 1999, https://www.washingtonpost.com/wp-srv/national/dotmil/arkin020199.htm.
4. Ibid.
5. Marc Ambinder, "Original Document: Making PSYOPS Less Sinister," *The Atlantic*, June 30, 2010, https://www.theatlantic.com/politics/archive/2010/06/original-document-making-psyops-less-sinister/58947/.
6. Ibid.
7. Jennifer Langston, "Lip-syncing Obama: New tools turn audio clips into realistic video," *UW News*, July 11, 2017, http://

www.washington.edu/news/2017/07/11/lip-syncing-obama-new-tools-turn-audio-clips-into-realistic-video/.

8. "Let's Get Experimental: Behind the Adobe MAX Sneaks," Adobe Blog, November 4, 2016, https://theblog.adobe.com/lets-get-experimental-behind-the-adobe-max-sneaks/.

9. Robert Hernandez, "Fake News and the Future of Journalism" TEDxKC, September 13, 2017, https://www.youtube.com/watch?v=4XGTTKJJsEw.

10. Michael Newberg, "As Many as 48 Million Twitter Accounts Aren't People, Says Study," CNBC, March 10, 2017, https://www.cnbc.com/2017/03/10/nearly-48-million-twitter-accounts-could-be-bots-says-study.html.

11. Lauren Smiley, "The College Kids Doing What Twitter Won't," *Wired*, November 1, 2017, https://www.wired.com/story/the-college-kids-doing-what-twitter-wont/.

12. "Botometer: An OSoMe project," https://botometer.iuni.iu.edu/#!/.

13. "Who, What, When, Where, Why, and How," *Columbia Journalism Review*, September 2013, https://archives.cjr.org/cover_story/who_what_when.php.

GLOSSARY

alternative fact A falsehood that contradicts truth and parades as fact.

bias Having favor for one thing or person than another thing or person, such as favoring Fox News over MSNBC.

bot An automated social media account that is programmed to help spread phony news.

conspiracy A covert plan by a person or group that aims to deceive or fool the masses.

digital media A mash-up of print and electronic media that uses computers, software, and networks to publish information.

disinformation Misinformation with the deliberate intent to deceive.

fourth estate Journalists and media organizations that aim to uphold democracy.

gaslighting A manipulation tactic that aims to persuade by making viewers distrust their own reality.

hoax A deceitful trick that aims to make a person believe something false to be true.

misinformation Incorrect information with the intention to spread false information, but sometimes is a product of sloppy reporting.

post-truth An instance when facts are less influential in public opinion than emotional fake news stories.

propaganda Biased information with the intent to persuade the reader or viewer to a particular viewpoint.

rumor A story or idea circulated that is rarely true, mostly false.

satire Using irony and humor to expose and roast political corruption or social foibles.

troll A person who sows discord by posting provocative comments on social media or in an online community.

yellow journalism Reporting that uses sensational misinformation to sell papers.

FURTHER READING

Books

Hand, Carol. *Everything You Need to Know About Fake News and Propaganda*. New York, NY: Rosen Young Adult, 2018.

McIntyre, Lee. *Post-Truth*. Cambridge, MA: MIT Press, 2018.

Schweitzer, Dahlia. *Going Viral: Zombies, Viruses, and the End of the World*. New Brunswick, NJ: Rutgers University Press, 2018.

Turkle, Sherry. *Alone Together: Why We Expect More from Technology and Less from Each Other*. New York, NY: Basic Books, 2017.

Websites

Center for Humane Technology
humanetech.com
The Center for Humane Technology is reversing the digital attention crisis and realigning technology with humanity's best interests.

Common Sense Media
www.commonsensemedia.org
Common Sense Media is the leading independent nonprofit organization dedicated to helping kids thrive in a world of media and technology.

MediaSmarts
mediasmarts.ca
MediaSmarts is a Canadian not-for-profit charitable organization for digital and media literacy.

INDEX